P9-CLR-016

ALL ASTURIAS
AND ITS PROVINCE

Text, lay-out and reproduction, entirely designed and created by the Technical Department of EDITORIAL ESCUDO DE ORO, S.A.

Photographs: F.I.S.A. in collaboration with Ediciones Alce.

Rights of total or partial reproduction and translation reserved.

Copyright of this edition for photographs and text: © EDITORIAL ESCUDO DE ORO, S.A.

1st Edition, February 1979

I.S.B.N. 84-378-0020-X

Esp. /Rúst. 84-399-7754-9	Esp. /Lujo 84-399-7755-7
Fran. /Rúst. 84-399-7756-5	Fran. /Lujo 84-399-7757-3
Ing. /Rúst. 84-399-7758-1	Ing. /Lujo 84-399-7759-X
Alem./Rúst. 84-399-7760-3	Alem./Lujo 84-399-7761-1

Dep. Legal B. 42726-XX

editorial **escudo de oro, s.a.** Palaudarias, 26 - Barcelona, 4 - Spain

Impreso en España - Printed in Spain

Vista de Cobadonga.

A view of Covadonga, the rugged place where Pelayo fortified himself againts the Moslems, from an old engraving.

The magnificent Cross of Victory which it is said was borne by Pelayo at Covadonga.

LAND OF THE RECONQUEST

Geography appears to have come to an agreement with history to make of Asturias both the redoubt from which Pelayo resisted the attacks of the Moslems, and the point where the first victorious impetus of the Reconquest originated. «In order to enter the heart of Asturias —said Ortega y Gasset— and to enter its territory, a Castilian must cross the Cantabrian mountain range via the passes at Leitariegos, Pajares, Piedrafita, el Pontón, Pan de Ruedas. The mountain passes, dear reader, are sublime, majestic places in lofty isolation. They are not of León-Castile, nor are they of Asturias. These are places to be chosen between the two. On either side of these mountain passes lie two completely different types of countryside guarding like the sheath of a sword two ways of life, two different and conflicting ways of accepting life».

But the land of Asturias was famous before Pelayo; it was where prehistoric man walked, as shown by the many remains found by scholars. In the prehistoric caves of Asturias at Penicial, Cueto de la Mina, Arnero, Ribadesella, la Franca, or Vidiago, among many others of similar interest, there is proof of the remote existence of a fishing folk culture, given the name of Asturiense, mixed with remains of other cultures such as the *Aziliense*, the higher milddle and lower *Magdaleniense*, the higher middle or lower *Solutrense,* the higher and middle *Auriñaciense* and the *Musteriense*. As remains of the prehistoric past of Asturias there are interesting cave paintings, megalithic monuments, bones, and the famous Peña Tu idol..

Asturias enters into the arena of history through its contact with Rome. After a long and valient struggle the Astures were conquered by the Romans in 19 B.C. and were obliged to abandon their hilltops

A night time view of the calle de Uría and the Plaza del Generalísimo in Oviedo.

and mountains to settle in the valleys. Thus, Publius Carisio, the first Roman prefect of *Asturias Trasmontana*, was assured that the bellicose Astures would not disrupt his government by fighting for the right to rule their homeland with their inborn independence of spirit. From the period of the Roman domination there remain monuments such as the Aras Sestianas at Gijón, fine mosaics like those at Vega del Ciego, funeral inscriptions at Naranco and Cornellana, votive altars, coins and also elements in the local folklore which are still alive as for example in the festivities of *el antruejo* and *los guirrios*.

The most glorious chapter in the history of Asturias is the fact that it became, with Pelayo and his hosts, both the land and the symbol of the Reconquest.

A handful of Goth guerrillas under the command of Pelayo, having escaped annihilation at the battle of Guadalete, succeeded in fortifying themselves at Covadonga and in restraining the hitherto irrisistible advance of Arab troops on Spanish soil.

The Astur monarchy, a historically important result of Pelayo's victorious resistence at Covadonga, soon became a nucleus of Christianity which not only communicated religious hope but was effective in uniting the will of the people and initiating the dynamic force of the Reconquest. For a long time, the church of Santa Cruz built at Cangas de Onís on an ancient megalithic sepulchral monument in the time of King Favila, the son and heir of Pelayo who was killed by a bear, was the temple and holy land of the Asturias. The young monarchy of Asturias was strengthened and glorified by Silo who transfered his court to Pravia, and by Fruela I and Alfonso II the Chaste who made Oviedo the captial of his kingdom.

A close-up of the pool in the Campo de San Francisco.

OVIEDO

Founded in the year 761 on the hill of Ovetao, the city began to grow around the monastery of San Vicente built by the abbot Fromestano, of Fromista; it is generally considered that Fruela I was the first monarch to instigate the development of Oviedo, However, «it was Alfonso II the Chaste, writes Dolores Medio, who, having settled some years later in this small town nucleus, began to develop the area». Alfonso «surrounded the small settlement with strong walls of which there are a few remains. He rebuilt some constructions begun by his father which had been either destroyed or abandoned during the reigns of Silo, Mauregato and Bermudo I. He had new buildings and churches constructed, thus creating the first examples of what was later to be called Asturian pre-Romanesque art».

Calle Uría, with the San Francisco gardens at one side.

View of the Cathedral of Oviedo, with its elegant tower, justifiably described as «a romantic poem in stone».

An evocative shot of the spacious cathedral cloister.

Other Asturian kings who contributed to the making of the city of Oviedo were Ramiro I who built the palace, the basilica of San Miguel, at the foot of Mount Naranco, and the hermitage of Santa Cristina de Lena; Alfonso III, the Great, during whose reign the churches at Tuñón, Goviendes, Priesca and Valdediós were built, and also a solid fortress; Fruela II also made other additions. When Alfonso IV established his court in León, the importance of Oviedo as a city began to decrease. Alfonso VI gave the city Municipal laws and Alfonso VII made it into a free city. But its leading role diminished and Oviedo became somewhat anonymous historically speaking. Nevertheless, it still played an important part especially in ecclesiastical and artistic matters during the Middle Ages, for in the Holy Coffers of Oviedo many religious relics and treasure was kept throughout the Mediaeval period.

Outstanding events in the history of Oviedo are the building of the cathedral, initiated towards the end of the XIV century, and the founding of the University in the XVII century.

THE CATHEDRAL

Constructed on the site occupied by the church built by Fruela I in the VIII century which was later razed by the Arabs and rebuilt by Alfonso II, the

A view of the richly adorned high altar in the Cathedral of Oviedo.

Detail of the rich ornamentation on the high altar.

The Annunciation, a sculpture appearing on the high altar.

The Adoration of the kings, another sculpture adorning the high altar of the cathedral.

The Cross of Oviedo, on show in the cathedral treasure room.

The most outstanding parts of the cathedral are the chapels of Santa Bárbara in churrigueresque style, and San Roque, dating from the beginning of the XVI century, the chapel of the Chaste King with three Romanesque heads above the portico, and the chapel of Los Vigiles; the transept with its fine baroque altar pieces, and the grandiose reredos in the main chapel considered along with those of Toledo and Seville to be one of the three most valuable in Spain.

The Holy Chamber, a jewel of Asturian pre-Romanesque architecture deserves a description of its own. The crypt is covered by a barrel vaulted ceiling. The nave rises up from three arches resting on three pillars at either side with the shaft of the columns decorated with figures of the twelve apostles sculpted in marble. The Holy Coffer contains, among other relics, the holy sudarium which it is said co-

The famous and artistic Cross of the Angels, one of the most prized jewels in the Holy Chamber.

cathedral was begun in the XIV century and finished in the XVI century being built almost exclusively during the course of the XV century. Its style is predominantly flamboyant Gothic and the building is made ip of three naves, the largest of these being 67 metres long, 10 metres wide and 20 metres in height. The fine cathedral tower which is the architectural pride of Oviedo was termed «a romantic poem in stone» by Leopoldo Alas and inspired Constantino Cabal, the Chronicler of Asturias in his native tongue to write these verses in praise of it:

> *Mio torre: torrina de aguyes de piedra*
> *qu'esguilen pel cielo lo mesmo que hiedra*
> *coyendoi a mantes cachinos de tul...*

The so-called coffer of the Calcedonias, a valuable possession of the cathedral of Oviedo.

A chest in embossed silver, a valuable part of the cathedral treasure.

vered the face of Jesus in the tomb, eight thorns from the crown given to Christ, a piece of the sheet in which the body of Christ is said to have been wrapped when in the tomb, a piece of Christ's tunic, a small phial with the blood shed in Syria by a crucified man wounded in side by the Jews, and several fragments of the Cross.

Among the art treasures kept in the Holy Chamber are, the Cross de los Angeles —donated to the cathedral by Alfonso II which appears on the coat of arms of Oviedo, the Cross de la Victoria - made from oak and precious stones, said to have been

A fine view of the door to the Holy Chamber.

carried by Pelayo at Covadonga, a Romanesque diptych dating from the XII century in silver and ivory, the Cristo Nicodemus - a XI century silver and ivory crucifix, several Byzantine crucifixes and a large number of small chests made of gold, silver and coral. The Gothic cloister is also of interest as well as the archives where important manuscripts and documents such as the *Book of the Testaments,* the *Book of the Regla Colorada* and the *Will of Alfonso II* are kept; the Diocescan Museum with its valuable IX, X, XI, and XII century archaeological pieces is also worthy of mention.

A close-up of the Holy Chamber in Oviedo cathedral.

The Nicodemus Christ, a lovely ivory and silver crucifix from the Holy Chamber.

A Byzantine diptych in ivory, a valuable piece belonging to the collection of works of art in the Holy Chamber.

The Holy Ark inside which priceless relics of the Passion of Christ are kept.

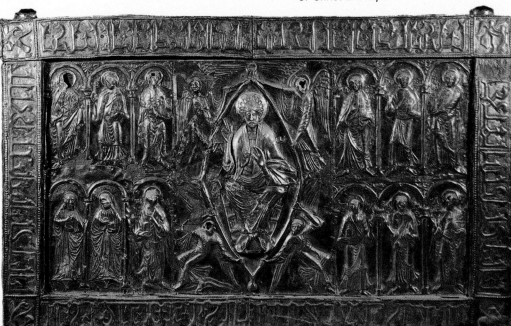

The tower on the palace housing the chambers of the council of Oviedo. ▷

The coat of arms of the city of Oviedo on the Town Hall.

THE TOWN HALL

Built initially in the year 1622 and reconstructed in 1780, it was modified in 1881 and extended in 1939. The palace has managed to preserve its original façade. The most outstanding feature of its architecture is the great archway belonging to the ancient Cimadevilla gate in the mediaeval wall. A lion sculpted in stone dominates the stairway leading from the lateral door which opens out at the end of a spacious arcade.

An impressive view of the elegant meeting chamber in the Town Hall of Oviedo.

A view of the attractive courtyard of Oviedo University.

THE UNIVERSITY

Situated in the centre of Oviedo, this building was begun in 1534, the year in which the university was founded by Fernando Valdés, and finished in 1608. It is a large solid building, square in shape, with interesting decoration on the doors and a fine cloister where there is a statue of the founder. The library has some valuable incunabulars and is of interest.

THE CITY

Oviedo is a distinctive city with an interesting history and defined cultural and human features. In his splendid novel *La Regenta*, the writer Clarín made a particularly penetrating study of the social context of the capital of Asturias. «Around the cathedral stretched the narrow area of the former precinct of Vetusta (Oviedo). This included what was known as

A view of the Plaza del Generalísimo, with the Palace of the Diputación in the distance.

A view of the façade of the Palace of the Diputación.

Partial view of the façade of the Valdecarzana palace.

Façade of the Campoamor Theatre, where important operas are performed.

the district of la Encimada (Cimadevilla) and dominated the whole village which had extended towards the northeast and the southeast. From the tower remains of the old city wall could be seen in courtyards and in the gardens of old houses in ruins, converted into mutual walls separating orchards and farmyards. La Encimada was both the noble district and the poor quarter of Vetusta. The highest born and the most beggarly lived here near together, the latter crowded together and the former more comfortably. The Oviedo described by Clarín still exists especially in the area around the cathedral. This part of Oviedo reaches the streets of Jovellanos, Azcárraga, Paraíso, Postigo Alto, Sol, and Ramón y Cajal, and the Plaza Mayor and the Plaza Porlier, a part

of the city with a definite human attractiveness, where there are many ancient palaces filled with the history of Asturias.

There is however another Oviedo, the modern, dynamic and progressive modern city growing in all directions with ultramodern buildings adding to the architecture. The nerve centres of the modern city are, la Escandalera, now the plaza del Generalísimo, the elegant and popular calle de Uría and el Campo de San Francisco. La calle Uría with its luxurious and modern cafés has the look of a boulevard of a big city. El Jardín or Campo de San Francisco is the green area of the city, an impressive green park measuring some 60.000 sq. metres in area, a peaceful place with pleasant lanes —los Curas, el Bombé,

*Façade of the
Camposagrado palace.*

*Façade of the old
Hospice, now converted
into a comfortable hotel.*

An evocative view of the cloister of the convent of San Vicente, now the Archaeological Museum.

los Alamos, and a romantic pool with swans and the popular Escorialín.

Oviedo is a city with pleasant facets. Firstly, the food here is extraordinarily good; the cider and Cabrales cheese —a cheese of a quality comparable to the best French ones— are certainly a gastronomic attraction. Also the famous *fabada Asturiana* (a casserole of beans with sausages) is a succulent dish; —in the words of the refrain: «with beans and cider petrol in not necessary». There are many bars and beamed inns filled with a jolly, outgoing clientele.

Oviedo has much to offer the sports enthusiast; there is the Royal Tennis Club, the Salinas Sailing Club, the Royal Automobile Club and the Carlos Tartiere Stadium. There are also several cultural institutions: the Opera season at Campoamor, the Capilla Polifónica, the Club Cultural, the Association of the Friends of Nature... etc.

The inhabitant of Asturias knows how to mix his natural joviality with a desiere for culture. As befits a city of ancient lineage, Oviedo has beeen able to establish a harmony between tradition and progress. It lives enjoying the present without forgetting the illustrious burden of its glorious past; and the legend on its coat of arms is particularly apt:

MOST NOBLE/ MOST LOYAL/ WORTHY UNCONQUERED/ HEROIC/ AND GOOD CITY/ OVIEDO.

The baroque altar in the church of Santa Teresa.

The façade of the Sanctuary of Nuestra Señora de las Cadenas.

A view of the palace of the Rúa, thought to be the oldest in Oviedo.

A panoramic view of the city of Oviedo, seen from the magnificent vantage point of the monte Naranco.

A fine view of the pre-Romanesque church of Santa María del Naranco. ▷

MONTE DEL NARANCO

Fine panoramic views of the capital of Asturias are to be seen from the heights of el Naranco. The road up the mountain has the added interest of being the official route to the pre-Romanesque buildings of the Palace of King Ramiro I, the church of St. Michael de Liño and the church of Santullano. This route begins leaving Oviedo by the calle de la Independencia (starting at Uría) going through the plaza de la Liberación and the calle del Teniente Tejeiro, where, at the end of this street, the calle de Ramiro I leads to the Avenida de los Monumentos. It is also possible to go from Independencia, the Arquitecto Marquina Viaduct, Avenida del Lago Enol, calle de Ramiro I and the Avenida de los Monumentos.

The Avenida de los Monumentos winds gaily up the mountain side by the luxuriant meadows and picturesque old houses on the slopes of el Naranco. Although the climb is steep, it is made easy by the impressive views to be seen all around.

On reaching the summit of el Naranco, the valley of Oviedo offers its charming multicoloured structure. The view is even more impressive if seen from the peaks of el Aramo, where there is the splendid sight of beautiful countryside reaching to the sea coast. This northen landscape, with its thousands of shades of green is impressively contrasted in the distance with the intensely blue strip of the Cantabrian sea.

THE PALACE OF KING RAMIRO

The palace is situated some two and a half two kilometres from the city on the slope of Naranco. This is indubitably one of the finest pre-Romanesque monuments in Asturias. Though forgotten for several centuries, it was declared a national monument in 1881. In 1931 it was restored and the additional buildings disfiguring its outline eliminated, being further restored in 1939.

The building belongs to the so-called Ramiran period, that is the second pre-Romanesque period. At the present time, it consists of two storeys, rectangular in shape one above the other. Of special note is the vast room divided into three precincts with cannon vaulted ceilings supported by plaster framed arches. The lateral columns supporting the arches are against the walls, joined together by the half pointed arches beautifully decorated with medallions and sculpted edges. Some fine views can be seen from the vindow of this room.

The lower floor is also devided into three precincts, one apparently meant to be a chapel, another a bathroom, and the third used for stables.

Built as a royal pleasure pavilion, it is constructed on the site of a former, probably Roman, edification.

A medallion carved in stone on the ancient walls of the Palace of Ramiro I.

A fine capital in the palace of Ramiro I.

SAN MIGUEL DE LIÑO

Situated a few metres away from the Palace of Ramiro and belonging to the same Ramiran pre-Romanesque period, this building has naves separated by arches supported by columns which in their turn are supported by square bases decorated with primitive figures; there is evident Byzantine influence in the decoration on the capitals.

Above the portal is a gallery with four doors having semicircular monolithic arches. The remains of mural paintings have been preserved on one of the walls and on what remains of the central nave. San Miguel de Liño was declared a national monument in 1885.

On one of the walls of the basilica of St. Michael de Liño are the remains of some sort of decoration in which it is possible to see a human figure seated on a purple coloured throne. The figure is drawn in profile, but with the face and arms facing forwards, looking at times like the figure of a woman. Behind the throne another smaller figure can be distinguished with arms and feet drawn in profile. According to the art expert Magín Berenguer, these figures belong to a scene from the Adoration of the Kings and are part of the Longobard repertory and were probably painted during the latter part of the VIII century.

On the eastern wall of the southern nave another figure of similar characteristics to the other two has been preserved. The yellow tone of the mantle and the purple background are still in a good state of preservation.

Close-up of the bell-tower of San Miguel de Liño.

One of the lovely windows of San Miguel de Liño.

Façade of the hermitage of Santullano.

Rear portion of the church and hermitage of Santullano.

A view of the interior of the hermitage of Santullano.

Mozarabic archways in the hermitage of Santullano.

Detail of the frescoes decorating the interior of the hermitage.

SAN JULIAN DE LOS PRADOS

Known also as the basilica de Santullano, this is the best preserved and most ancient monument of the Asturian pre-Romanesque period. It consists of three naves and a transept decorated with wood. The head of the church is rectangular in shape and has three cannon vaulted chapels. The inside of the church is remarkable in that it is decorated with a profusion of fine pictures; an outstanding painting is one of the cross in ochre with the letters alpha and omega. San Julián de los Prados is also a national monument.

A general view of the winter resort of Valgrande.

PUERTO DE PAJARES

It is an exciting visual experience to come into Asturias through the Puerto de Pajares. Suddenly the monotony of the Castilian landscape is interrupted by the appearance of a craggy spot full of impressive majesty. «To enter into Asturias, says Eugenio Nadal, is to find oneself suddenly in a world alone, cut off. Puerto de Pajares —vertical unassailable: an immense amphitheatre of mountains with sheer green slopes looms over dark valleys lost in the deep: a damp mist obscures outlines in the foothills where from time to time a cow bell rings, peaceful and out of tune; nearby a waterfall tumbles down noisy and cool, far ahead red-roofed houses can be seen almost falling from the steep slope... Houses and villages stretch into the interior of Asturias. Valleys and mountains, woods and rivers, meadows and cultivated land come in succession. Then there appears the mining area and afterwards the green panorama of the valley of Oviedo and the river Nalón.

As Ortega y Gasset says in his *Notas de ver y andar,* —«the first unwary look we take from Pajares to the other side is always a visual failure. The cornea is hampered by a substance similar to cotton wool which makes it unable to discern any route: this is the mist, the neverending mist that comes in whiffs like a deep breath from the valley below.»

*Close-up of
the winter
resort of
Valgrande.*

An evocative view of the Puerto de Pajares, with the road in the foreground.

A beautiful panoramic view of the Puerto and the village of Pajares.

Façade of the hermitage of Santa Cristina at Pola de Lena.

MIERES

Mieres is the most important city in the centre of Asturias and is the capital of the mining region with its rivers Nalón and el Caudal. The town is so built that, in the words of Víctor Alperi «all the streets end in the mountains». The socio-economic life of Mieres revolves round the «Factory», a steel works of the first order which gave rise to the growth of the city from the middle of the XIX century. At the present time the mines now worked have united under the name of HUNOSA.

COLLOTO

Colloto is situated on the road from Oviedo to Santander and is surrounded by lovely countryside especially in the area around the river Nora. The village has a fine XII century Romanesque church named Santa Eulalia, which has an impressive triumphal arch and capitals. Another important monument is the Roman bridge over the river Nora. There is also a brewery.

NOREÑA

A village of ancient lineage as shown by the fact that the bishops of Oviedo still use the honorary title of counts of Noreña. The village grew up around the ancient castle and is an important industrial and agricultural centre. Among its most outstanding monuments are the palaces of Miraflores, Los Llanes and el Rebollín, as well as the XVII century church with its excellent baroque altar pieces.

A close-up of the lovely Jovellanos Park at Mieres.

LA FELGUERA

This is an industrial mining town divided by the course of the river Nalón from its rival Sama; La Felguera has the look of a town influenced by the dynamic working spirit of its inhabitants and by its sporting proclivities. The railway joining the Langreo valley to Gijón begins in the town. The writer Azorín, a keen observer, was able to capture the subtlety of the mining landscape: «As night draws near, the train runs along the edge of the black waters of the Nalón, sometimes noisily crossing a metal bridge, and in the distance are the lights of a village».

SAMA DE LANGREO

A mining town par excellence like La Felguera, Sama is the capital of the municipality of Langreo, and lives from the mines and industries derived from coal. In the initial stages of the Asturian monarchy it was royal land, later belonging to the bishopric of Ovie-

Two partial views of Mieres, an important mining town.

A general view of the dynamic mining town of La Felguera.

do having been ceded by Alfonso VI; Philip II claimed it once more for the crown in 1575 but seven years later the council acquired its independence.

RIOSECO AND EL NALON

There are various monuments of great interest near to Rioseco: el Castillo —a Roman tower at Villamorey—, the Roman arch near to Pola de Laviana over the river Nalón, —the hermitage of La Magdalena, and the church of Santa María with its pre-Romanesque remains. The waters of the river Nalón have increased and become rich with trout. This idyllic landscape watered by the river Nalón is the background for the novel by Palacio Valdés entitled *La aldea perdida.*

INFIESTO

Many Roman and prehistoric remains were found in the area surrounding the town, but the first historical dates related to Infiesto come from the mediaeval times. At the present time, it is a pleasant spot with equally engaging scenery having an important fish factory and possessing a dynamic agricultural centre. Near to the town there is a sanctuary which comes out of a rock called the Virgin de la Cueva that inspired the popular verse:

> *Que llueva, que llueva,*
> *Oh, Virgen de la Cueva.*
> *Los pajaritos cantan,*
> *las nubes se levantan...*

CANGAS DE ONIS

This is an historic town where Pelayo established his court after vanquishing the Arabs at the battle of Covadonga. It was the capital of the Asturian monarchy until Alfonso II the Chaste transfered the court to Oviedo.

Situated on the spurs of land belonging to the Picos de Europa, the town is surrounded by magically beautiful scenery and its streets have many fine aristocratic mansions. The ancient lineage of Cangas de Onís is shown by the existence of a fine Roman bridge.

An original shot of the Roman bridge at Cangas de Onís.

COVADONGA

According to tradition, Pelayo, having been elected king on the battle field, received breath from the Virgin who appeared to the Christian warriors in the same spot where at the present time the sanctuary of Covadonga is situated; Covadonga meaning *Cova-longa* or *long cave.* Tradition also has it that even before the Arab invasion the Virgin was worshipped in this grotto which is an opening in a high rock under which there falls a torrential stream first stopping at el Pozón and later becoming a tiny stream. On the left of this torrent there is a fountain and its

Statue erected at Covadonge to Don Pelayo.

View of the Basilica of Covadonga with the mountains in the background.

waters, according to popular legend, possess the property of bringing happiness and marriage to those who drink there.

The popular statue of la Santina, now substituted for a modern one as the former was destroyed by fire in the XVIII century, presides over the holy cave which is reached by a staircase with more than a hundred steps which many pilgrims climb on their knees, or by a tunnel hewn out of the rock at the end of which are the tombs of Pelayo and Alfonso I. At the foot of the cave is the collegiate church of St. Ferdinand, the cloister being the only remaining part of the original building. Building was begun on the new catheral in 1887 and it was inaugurated in 1901; there is a rich treasure in its interior including the crowns of the Virgin and Child and other religious objects.

The statue of *La Santina,* as the Asturians affectionately call their Virgin, is in polychromed wood, and the affectionate nickname of *Santina* is due to its size which is smaller than usual in statues of this kind. In the words of the popular verse:

> *La Virgen de Covadonga*
> *es pequeñina y galana.*
> *Ni que bajara del cielo*
> *el pintor que la pintara.*

Convadonga is the centre of numerous pilgrimages coming, not only from Asturias, but from the most diverse parts of the Iberian peninsula. The situation of the sanctuary is one of extraordinary beauty, being a steep rugged place of unique natural contours.

On the esplanade of the Cathedral are the seminary, the house of retreat, the chapter house, the modern ecclesiastical residences, hotels for the tourists and tourist services, and the Post Office.

The centre of the square is dominated by a statue of Don Pelayo —the hero of the Reconquest—, by the sculptor Zaragoza.

The Holy Cave of Covadonga.

Statue of the Virgin of Covadonga, the popular patroness of Asturias.

A group of mountaineers in the Picos de Europa.

THE PICOS DE EUROPA

The colossal mountain mass is one of the most characteristic and most impressive sights in the Asturian landscape. From these peaks several streams descend to irrigate the land on the plains below. The view from here is an extraordinary and unforgettable experience and quite unique. The Picos de Europa form part of the Cantabrian mountain range and stretch along the provinces of Santander, Asturias and León. Until fairly recently the imposing rocks on the summit had not been touched by a living soul. «Such is their beauty and majesty, states the Asturian writer Dolores Medio, that one becomes speechless with admiration on contemplating them. Words are superfluous. I would say that it is impssible even to describe them. They must be admired in religious silence while totally immersing oneself in the beauty of the landscape.

One should imagine oneself an eagle, flying high and leaving the minutiae of daily life away down in the valleys and soaring up to the heights again looking towards the heavens. The solitude of the place, its infinite peace occasionally perturbed by the

Sturdy rocks dominate the summit of the Picos de Europa.

The majestic presence of the Naranco de Bulnes a peak situated in the central mass of the Picos de Europa.

unexpected leap of an ibex fleeing from man, tone up the spirit and leave it clean with the cold clear water of its springs».

The Picos de Europa can be reached by roads coming from the land of Asturias, from the nearby lands of Santander, or the neighbouring province of León. The roads leading to the peaks are adorned with extraordinarily lovely villages with charming personalities, such as Arenas de Cabrales, Poncebos, Panes — the capital of Peñamera Baja, a town situated in the foothills of the Sierra de Cuera, near to Deva, a real hunters' and fishermen's paradise, Potes, Turieno, Camaleño, Mogroveito, Cosgaya, Espinama, Pido...

The «North Face» of the Naranco de Bulnes, some 2.519 metres in height.

At Fuente-Dé, where the river Deva has its source, there is a Tourist Inn and the first cable car in the Picos de Europa which stretches to the vantage point of Lloroza, where there are some unforgettable panoramic views. Not far from Lloroza is the sanctuary of Aliva where the hermitage of the Virgin de las Nieves and the rustic palace, used by the kings and princess of Spain for spending the night during their hunting parties in the craggy area, offer an enormous tourist attraction.

Among the Picos de Europa there are some of considerable height, such as Tabla de Lechugales, 2.445, Pico Fierro 2.426, Tiro de la Infanta 2.430, Naranco de Bulnes 2.519, and Torre Cerredo and El Neverón.

An impressive close-up of the «South Face» of the Naranco de Bulnes.

A general view of Llanes, with the clear blue of the Cantabrian sea in the background.

The town of Llanes viewed from the sea, surrounded by its fertile meadows.

PIMIANGO, COLOMBRES, VILLANUEVA...

This is a coastal area with many prehistoric caves like the one of the same name on the magnificent beach of La Franca or el Pindal at Pimiango where there are some valuable cave paintings. Nearby is the San Emeterio lighthouse, the Tina Mayor estuary and the ruins of the XII century monastery of Santa Ana de Tina. The surrounding countryside is particularly lovely in Colombres, where Carlos I stayed, and in Villanueva with its Torre de los Noriega and several manorial houses of much interest.

LLANES

This is an exceptionally lovely place and the nucleus of the most important village in the eastern part of Asturias. Numerous prehistorical remains have been found in its environs, and in the Middle Ages the district of Llanes was given the name «lands of Aguila», which derives from Aguilar, the surname of the lords who owned the area. The town was walled during the reign of Alfonso IX who gave it a statute. Llanes is quite rich in monuments, and has still kept a large part of its wall and many buildings dating from the same period and from the Renaissance. The XII century Romanesque-Gothic transition parish church of Santa María is very interesting, and other monuments of similar interest are: la Casa de las Sirenas, the monastery of the Augustinas Recoletas and the house in the calle Mayor where Charles I stayed.

Worthy of mention is the picturesque quayside area, and not far from Llanes is the Cué aerodrome, the third largest in Asturias.

A view of the attractive Sablón Beach at Llanes.

A superb
close-up of
the natural
rock formation
known as
«The profile of
Christ»
situated on
the coast near
to Llanes.

A lovely view of the fishing port of Llanes.

An aerial view of Poo, a particularly lovely spot near to Llanes.

A fine view of Celorio.

A shot of the María Elena camping site at Celorio.

The beach and water sports quay at Celorio.

A lovely close-up of the beach at Celorio.

A general view of Barro, a beach close to Llanes.

A magnificent close-up of the port of Lastres with the village in the background.

The Town Hall and the Plaza del Generalísimo at Villaviciosa.

POSADA

The village is the ideal centre for visiting such places as San Antolín de Bedón where there is a fine Benedictine monastery in late Romanesque style dating from the XIII century, or picturesque places on the coast such as Niembro or Barro. Also nearby is the enchanting beach of Cuevas de Mar the impressive megalithic monument of Peña-Tu, the caves at Bricia, Fonfría, Barro and Lledias, the latter being decorated with valuable cave paintings.

RIBADESELLA

The last of the seven towns on the Costa Verde, Ribadesella is located on the edge of the river Sella which is famous for its sports competions of international class celebrated along its course and due to the abundance of salmon and trout found in its waters. The river divides the village into two: the old Ribadesella with its more recent constructions, its hotels, cafés, on the one hand and the large bridge joining the village with its splendid beach on the other. Many prehistoric remains have been found in the environs of Ribadesella, mostly in the caves of San Antonio, Ardines, Las Pedroses, El Cierro and La Cuevona; there are also some Roman remains. This village also played an important part during the history of the Middle Ages.

There are some old houses and the fine Renaissance palace of the Prieto-Cutre among the outstanding monuments in Ribadesella.

The canoeing festivities and the international descent of the river Sella give the town a jovial atmosphere which is increased by the presence of animated groups of choirs and popular dancers.

A general view of Villaviciosa, a lovely town in the middle of idyllic countryside.

A typical Asturian granary in the district of Villaviciosa.

VILLAVICIOSA

This is the fourth most important town on the Costa Verde and has been known by its present name since the end of the XIII century. Strabo mentions the lovely estuary of Villaviciosa as being the limit between the transmontane Asturians and the Selene Cantabrians, and the town is often alluded to by various names: *Maliaio, Maiayo, Malayo* in mediaeval documents. There are many remains which speak of its possible Roman origin —monuments, coins, etc. found in the environs of Villaviciosa. Though the town was destroyed by fire in the XV century, it was rebuilt and ennobled by Charles I due to the fact that he disembarked at the nearby village of Tazones. The countryside surrounding the village is exceptionally lovely, and is enthusiastically complimented in the popular verse:

A fine view of Villaviciosa and the lovely countryside around the town.

The front of the elegant church of Santa María.

*Villaviciosa hermosa
qué llevas dentro,
que me robas el alma
y el pensamiento...*

In Villaviciosa there are innumerable houses with aristocratic coats of arms and among its monuments the following are outstanding: the church of Santa María in transitional Romanesque Gothic style, the former monastery of San Francisco, now the parish church, the monument to the Apple by Benlliure, and the house where the Emperor stayed in 1517. Especially worthy of mention are the nearby pre-Romanesque churches of San Salvador de Valdediós, San Salvador de Priesca and Santiago de Gobiendes and the marvellous Romanesque church of San Juan de Amandi situated one kilometre from Villaviciosa.

An artistic close-up of the church of Valdediós, a pre-Romanesque church situated amid impressive scenery.

A general view of the monastery of Valdediós with the countryside in the background reaching gently up the slopes of the mountains.

A general view of Tazones with the port in the foreground.

Evening in the port of Tazones.

A general view of the impressive San Lorenzo beach at Gijón.

GIJON

This city is the most densely populated in Asturias, and according to Juan Cueto Alas, just as Oviedo is the cultural and administrative centre in winter, Gijón takes on this same role during the summer season, not only for matters concerning the beach, but because during the summer months Asturians flee en masse to the coast and Gijón is the most important place on it».

It is certain that the city played an important part during the period of Roman domination; the existence of Roman baths would appear to emphasize this, and the first mention of Gijón after this is in the year 857 when a donation made by Ordoño I is refe-

red to. The name of Gijón then appears in matters related to Alfonso III the Great, Juan I, and el Rey Sabio. The city took the side of Enrique de Trastámara count of Gijón and Noreña, against King Pedro the Cruel. The city then went through a period of singular misfortune when it was set fire to at the orders of the wife of Alfonso Enríquez before being handed over to Enrique III, who, in his turn, ordered the city to be razed and for it to be incorporated into the crown. In the XV century the wounds inflicted on the city of Gijón began to heal and the Catholic Monarchs (Ferdinand and Isabella) approved a project for the construction of a port at Gijón. Three centuries later, Gijón was the coastal capital of Asturias and the city became an important industrial and mercantile centre.

A view of the magnificent quayside at Gijón.

An aerial view of the quayside at Gijón.

Monument to the Mother of the Emigrant erected facing the port of Gijón.

A night time view of the inner port of Gijón.

THE ROMAN BATHS

The baths occupy an area of some 960 metres and consist of two buildings; they are situatead near the cerro de Santa Catalina, at the point known by the name of Campo de Valdés. The best preserved is the smaller one, decorated with paintings on the friezes and skirting boards. These date from the Ist century A.D: and were discovered in 1903.

THE CITY

At the present time Gijón has the air of a large city —modern, industrial, and with the added dimension of a tourist attraction. In spite of all this, the city has still been able to conserve its lordly personality along with its popular image.

This is the lovely city of Jovellanos —don Gaspar Melchor was born here in the middle of the XVIII century in the district of Cimadevilla and he is possibly one of Gijón's most illustrious sons and also one who did the most to make it great.

There are many old palaces to be found along the streets of Gijón, one dating from the Renaissance belonging to the Marquis de San Esteban, the Casa de las Recoletas and the tower of the Jove-Hevia, also three fine churches —la Colegiata, built in 1702 and later restored, the chapel of San Lorenzo de Tierra and San Lorenzo de Mar, and in the lovely

A close-up of the Gijón Regatta Club.

A splendid panoramic view of the beach of San Lorenzo, situated at the foot of the city.

A view of the Paseo de San Lorenzo in Gijón.

The San Lorenzo beach with the motor way in the foreground.

A general view of the mouth of the river Piles on the San Lorenzo beach.

A view of the San Lorenzo beach.

Close-up of the San Lorenzo beach with the outline of the ultramodernen buildings surrounding it in the background.

Plaza Mayor one can pass the time under the porches near to the Municipal Palace.

In spite of the importance of the port, the quayside has kept its popular appeal and is a sort of prolongation of the Cimadevilla district. The port facilities are excellent. Gijón has three industrial ports altogether —Fomentín, Fomento and Musel— and also a fishing port. The quayside at Gijón is dynamic and popular with its picturesque taverns and constant bustle of sailors, fishermen, and carriers, all very reminiscent of the picture reflected by the Asturian novelist Armando Palacio Valdés in his work *La alegría del Capitán Ribot.*

In the cultural sphere there are two outstanding institutions of great importance in the social life of Gijón: the Instituto Jovellanos, founded by Jovellanos himself in 1794, and the Labour University which occupies an enormous building decorated by famous artists with really splendid facilities inside.

The San Lorenzo beach, the finest seaside resort for summer holidaymakers is the loveliest and most popular beach on the whole Costa Verde. Its impresive sandy beach stretches for two kilometres from Campo Valdés to the river Piles where there are a great many popular picnic spots.

At the end of Campo Valdés, a short avenue where

A view of the aristocratic palace with the statue to Don Pelayo before it.

An endearing view of the picturesque district of Cimadevilla.

the Roman hot springs are situated, on the same side as the escarpment, is the church of San Pedro, already quoted by Alfonso X when in 1270 he donated to the monastery of San Vicente de Oviedo «Our church of the Town of Gijón which we order to be made in Asturias», specifying in another document two years later «that they be parishioners of the church known as San Pedro who have San Salvador in the Town of Gijón». The original church was razed by a great fire at the end of the XIV century. In the year 1400, a royal decree from king Enrique III ordered the rebuilding of the city, and with it, that of the

church of San Pedro. It was later restored during the XVI, XVIII, and XIX centuries, and though destroyed during the civil war, was rebuilt in 1945. In Campo Valdés is the palace of don Fernando Valdés, who gave his name to the place, governor of the province and perpetual alderman of Oviedo and Gijón, chief ensign of Villaviciosa and sergeant major of the Principality. The palace was built in the XVIII century on a Roman wall surrounding the old city and occupies the same situation as the Torre Augusta which was destroyed by fire. This fine palace has two elegant towers decorated with plateresque motifs. Joined to

Close-up of the Plaza de José Antonio in Gijón.

View of the Plaza de los Mártires.

the palace is the chapel of the Virgin of Guadalupe whose architecture blends in perfect harmony.

Campo Valdés serves as an urban anteroom to the enchanting district of Cimadevilla. This fishing quarter, with its steep little streets was the birthplace of don Gaspar Melchor de Jovellanos. Here in a charming nearby square bordering Campo Valdés is the palace, built in the XVI century, where Jovellanos was born. The building is now a museum and Centre for Jovellanist studies, and inside are books and manuscripts relating to Jovellanos and reminiscences of the illustrious Asturian. Some of the rooms in the museum are devoted to the history of Gijón, mining, archaeology and a special library for newspapers and magazines.

Next to the palace of Jovellanos, built in a similar style of elegant sobriety is the chapel of Nuestra Señora de los Remedios and on one of the side walls next to the Epistle is the tomb of don Melchor de Jovellanos whose head stone was designed by Inclán-Valdés. The nineteenth century poets Quintana and Juan Nicasio Gallego wrote the epitaph.

Aerial view of the sports installations and football field of Molinón.

An aerial view of the locale for the Asturias National Samples Fair and the Ethnological Museum «Pueblo de Asturias».

An aerial view of the Gijón camping site.

Partial view of the Labour University with its swimming pool in the foreground.

Stained glass in the chapel of the Labour University at Gijón.

Central courtyard of the Labour University at Gijón.

An aerial view of Perlora.

Partial view of Candás with the port in the foreground.

View of the beach at Candás.

Slope up to the church of el Cristo de Candás.

CANDAS

This is one of the most important fishing villages in Asturias. Here there are many large tinning factories, and this was the place where the action of the novel *José*, was situated, written by Palacio Valdés and later made into a film.

This evocative village on the Costa Verde appears to contemplate its own image like Narcissus in the waters of the sea. The church of San Felix is of interest with its baroque altar piece of the Christ of Candás whose image was picked up, according to legend, when floating on the water near the coast of Ireland. In honour of this saint popular festivities are celebratet during the first days of September dedicated to love, as the following verse states:

> *Fui al Cristo y enamoréme.*
> *Malhaya la namorá.*
> *Fui al Cristo y enamoréme,*
> *Morena mía.*
> *No te podré olvidar.*
> *Malhaya la namorá.*

Aerial view of Candás with the blue sea as a back drop.

Aerial view of the town of Luanco.

A lovely close-up of the wharf at Luanco.

A general view of Luanco.

A charming view of the lovely port of Luanco.

LUANCO

This is one of the seven towns on the Costa Verde and the main town of the municipality of Gozón. Luanco was already in existence in Roman times. It is a fishing port and a summer holiday resort. It has an interesting parish church with three valuable baroque altar pieces, and there is the Palace of the Menéndez-Pola and the Asturias Maritime Museum.

The façade of the mansion of los Pola with its characteristic eaves and balconies.

A view of the lovely walk in Luanco.

A view of the port at Luanco.

The beach at Luanco with the port in the background.

◁ *A fine close-up of the cliffs of the Cabo Peñas.*

A partial view of Avilés.

AVILES

This town still conserves, in the old part of its urban limits, remains of its ancient past (the town being already in existence in Roman times) and is at the present time one of the most industrialized and densely populated centres in Spain.

During the Middle Ages, Avilés, played an outstanding part historically. Alfonso VI granted the town a statute, kept in the Municipal Archives, towards the end of the XI century which was confirmed by Alfonso VII at the end of XII century. El Rey Sabio gave the town further privileges and declared Avilés exempt of tolls in Oviedo.

Time seems to have stood still in the old part of town of Avilés with its irregular streets, steep and

narrow, some with porticos. Among its monuments the following are outstanding: —the palace of Camposagrado with its baroque façade topped by an enormous coat of arms, the old parish of San Nicolás, now a Fransican residence with a restored doorway dating from the XII century, the chapel of Los Alas dating from the XIV century with seven fine Gothic reliefs in the interior, the house of the Baragañas, also known as the palace of the Valdecarzana from the XV century, and the Town Hall building occupying one of the sides of the Plaza de España with its noble Herreran façade topped by a bell tower.

The Plaza de España or Plaza Mayor as it is popularly known is the nerve centre of Avilés, from here seven roads branch out, some towards the river estuary where they make a pleasant contribution to

A splendid view of the church of San Francisco.

A close-up of the port.

Panoramic view of the Salinas beach.

the beauty of the city. Other streets of interest are Suárez-Inclán, Pinar del Río, the former Ferrería, los Alas or Ruiz Gómez at the corner of which the Palacio Valdés Theatre is situated. The first stone of this theatre was laid by another illustrious Asturian Leopoldo Alas in the year 1900.

Other points of interest are the Marqués de Teverga street which stretches from the busy calle de la Cámara to the very edge of the estuary and ends with a typical Avilesian market, also the streets of Florida and Pedro Menéndez leading to the picturesque district of the fishermen where the XII century Romanesque church of Santo Tomás is situated in the calle del General Zubillaga.

Mention must be made of the large factory ENSIDE-SA, which provided an impulse for the extraordinary industrial boom of modern Avilés. The installation of this industrial complex of the first order lent momentum to the present day development of this fine progressive city and increased its labour population considerably.

Another important aspect of Avilés is its port. This, even in the Middle Ages, was the most important in Asturias.

There is also the airport of Asturias situated beside the picturesque village of Ranón, and the beaches at Arnao, El Cuerno and Santa María, all of them on the coastline of Avilés.

An aerial view of Avilés with the arm of the estuary reaching inland.

A partial view of Salinas,
an important summer
resort in Asturias.

Aerial view of the Santa
María del Mar beach.

EL PITO

A picturesque seaside town where the Selgas palace stands —a nineteenth century building housing an important museum with frescoes, pictures by Goya and El Greco and a fine collection of XVI century tapestries.

PRAVIA

This town was of some importance in Roman times and during the Middle Ages. At the present time it is a fine prosperous town with an impressive urban structure and is the centre of a large agricultural and cattle rearing area. Among its more outstanding monuments are: the parish church, a former collegiate church, the Moutas palace, the Town Hall and the hermitage of the Virgen del Valle dating from the XIV century where a fine Renaissance altar piece is kept along with an artistic polychromed carving of the Virgin.

Near to Pravia is San Román de Candamo with its famous prehistoric cave of La Peña and the lovely palace of the Valdés Bazán; there is also the village of Santianes, where King Silo held his court, with a pre-Romanesque basilica and several mansions.

A fine close-up of the port of Luarca.

Partial view of the town of Luarca.

A general view of the port of Luarca.

LUARCA

This is a picturesque white town situated at the mouth of the river Negro rich in trout and eels; the river divides Luarca in two unequal parts and has seven bridges. Luarca is one of the loveliest seaside towns on the Asturian coast and has three magnificent beaches which constitute a great tourist attraction.

Interesting monuments in this town are the X century parish church, the palace of the marquis de Ferrara dating from the XIV century, the house of the Gamoneda, from the XVIII century and the old Town Hall building. The ancient and picturesque fishing quarter is also very interesting, and another attractive district is Cambaral.

A panoramic view of the sheltered port of Luarca.

The Cambaral area has an interesting history. Its name, according to popular tradition, comes from that of the pirate Kamboral who was apparently the one who killed the knight don Teudo de Villademoros. Another legend belonging to the area alludes to the frequent devastating landings of the Normans in the middle of the IX century.

At the present time, the area of Cambaral, which is reached by the street of the same name that leads to the promontory of La Atalaya, is particularly picturesque in structure. Here is the plaza de la Mesa (Table Square) around which, since mediaeval times, the ancient council of Luarca, and in the XIX century, the «Most noble Guild of Seamen and Navigators, gentlemen of Loarca», met to discuss matters related to the guilds, the price of salt, the annual projects of the whaling companies or the content of the ancient Royal Decrees requested to combat the Moors or the heretics.

Here in this quarter is a monument representing fourteen important episodes in the history of Luarca.

Worthy of special mention is the hermitage of La Blanca, situated not far from the cemetery and of great popularity in Luarca. This was erected in honour of the Virgin, who, in November 1530, according to tradition, appeared in the grotto of La Blanca.

A view of Luarca by night, with its profuse illumination.

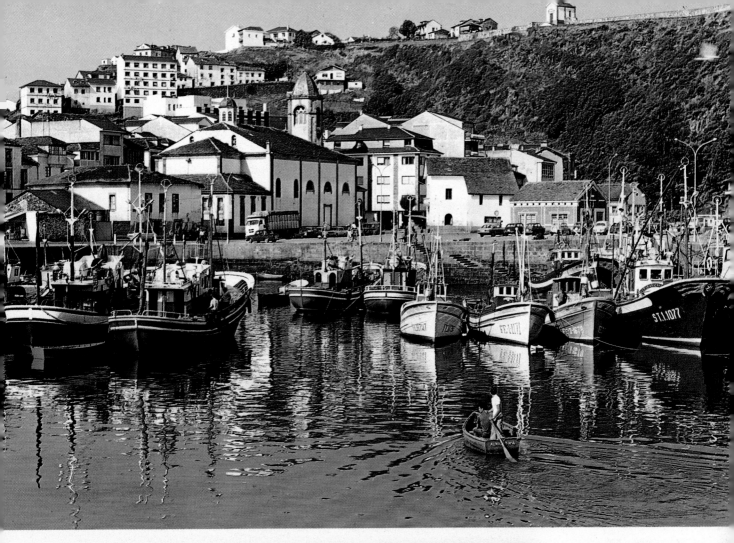

Another view of the attractive port of Luarca.

Close-up of the Plaza del Ayuntamiento, with the Town Hall building in the background.

Partial view of the lovely town of Navia.

NAVIA

The town is situated at the mouth of the river of the same name whose origin is described as follows by the writer Camilo José Cela: «There where men live and love and govern themselves and die as they did at the beginning of the centuries, there in the old land of Lugo, in the ancient mountain of Cebrero, a young and singing Navia is born which swells and grows by Navia de Suarna and the mountain ranges of el Busto, Piedras Apañadas and San Roque to water, as it falls, the town of Navia...» The town is possibly of Roman origin and was of some importance during the Middle Ages. There are still many palaces and aristocratic mansions showing Navia's historic tradition.

A view of the river Navia; at the mouth of this river is the town of the same name.

Ruins of the Celtic village of Loaña.

A general view of Tapia de Casariego.

An aerial view of Tapia de Casariego.

An impressive close-up of the port of Tapia de Casariego.

A splendid panoramic view of Figueras with the sea stretched out like a blue carpet at its feet.

CASTROPOL

Sited on the top of a promontory, the town is built like a castle cum watch tower on the beautiful estuary of the Eo, opposite the land of Galicia. Castropol is one of the quietest and most secluded of Asturian towns, with its old palaces, its lonely little squares and white houses with slate roofs. It is like a lovely balcony over the river estuary. Intersting places to visit are the chapel of Nuestra Señora del Campo dating from the XV century, the church of Santiago, and the palaces of Montenegro and Valledor.

Numerous excursions can be taken from Castropol —to the end of the estuary on the other side of which is the Galician town of Ribadeo—, to Villanueva de los Oscos. Tapia de Casariego, Santa María de los Oscos and Santa Eulalia de los Oscos, where the Marquis de Sargadelos was born who, at the end of the XVIII century, created the famous porcelaine factory which bears his name.

Partial view of the lovely town of Castropol, with the estuary in the background.

CANGAS DE NARCEA

The primitive ovens, coins and other remains found in the proximities of Cangas de Narcea show that the Romans were there for some time. Cangas is an attractive town with old palaces among them the one belonging to the Queipo de Llano family which is now the town hall, the XVI century Omaña palace and churches such as Santa María Magdalena dating from the XVII century, and the monastery of Corias, called «the Escorial of Asturias».

TINEO

This town is located on the side of the mountain of the same name and is surrounded by singularly lovely countryside. The old part of Tineo is especially attractive with its lovely old irregular streets and the XIII century parish church in Romanesque — Gothic transitorial style, the fine Gothic palace of the Maldonado and Campomanes, the palace of los Meras and the ancient pilgrims' hospital with is remians of mediaeval paintings. In the modern part of Tineo one's attention is attracted by the numerous bars restaurants where the best known dishes to be tasted are, ham, salmon and the trout fished nearby.

GRADO

This town is built on the site of a former Roman settlement, and had a turbulent existence in the Middle Ages. From its glorious past there remain parts of castles, palaces and mansions. Not far from Grado is the XII century Romanesque church of Santa Eulalia de la Mata, where the bishop Adulfo lies buried, also the XII century Romanesque church of San Martín de Gurullés and the mediaeval tower at Coalla.

Close-up of the statue to Villaamil in Castropol.

ASTURIAN GASTRONOMY

This land offers good food and drink and a wide choice of tasty dishes among then being: the famous *fabada* (bean stew) and its most popular variant *el pote asturiano* (soup), los *arbeyos* (peas) with ham and a wide variety of soups. Not forgetting the succulent *caldereta* and an infinity of fish dishes: hake done with cider or *a la antigua,* with asparagus tips and green peas, sea-bream, sardines, trout, salmon, etc. and a great variety of shell-fish.

A meat dish worthy of mention is the beef stew with calf's foot, pork, onions, turnips, herbs, pepper and wine.

For dessert any Asturian chesse is good, but the cheese from Cabrales is a speciality; and in sweets, the popular rice with milk which originated here in Asturias.

The very popular, slightly acid cider is recommended to drink as it is deliciously refreshing and digestive.

The delicious Asturian «fabada» one of the outstanding dishes in the Spanish gastronomic repertory.

ASTURIAN FOLKLORE

The folklore of this region is one of the oldest, richest and most picturesque in Spain. The Corri-Corri is probably the oldest dance there is. This is a fecundating dance which at the present time is danced, in Cabrales, with six women and a man who with their jumps and twists simulate the eternal rites of love. The traditional cowherds dances are also very old, these are danced to the music of the *payetsa*, a sort of frying pan whose handle is furnished with an enormous key. The bag pipes and the timbrel are, as in Galicia, very characteristic instruments of the whole of the region of Asturias. A festival of great antiquity is that of the cowherds of Alzada patronized by the Ministry of Information and Tourism; the most attractive facet of this festivity is when a wedding party is accompanied on horseback to the chapel in the pasture ground with people singing popular verses alluding the theme of marriage:

> *Aqui van lus de la boda*
> *todus llevan vestíu negru,*
> *menos la señora novia,*
> *que viene de terciopelo.*

After the ceremony there is much dancing and cowherd songs are sung, then the festivities end with a picnic.

Among the many traditonal Asturian celebrations, an outstanding one is celebrated in the sanctuary of the Virgen del Viso on August 15th, there is also the Festival de la Manzana de Nava, the pilgrimage to Carmín de Siero, the Fiesta de las Comadres on Carnival Tuesday and the festival of Los Huevos Pintos celebrated on the first Tuesday after Easter Sunday.

Two Asturians dressed in the typical regional costume.

Asturians dressed in regional costume rehearse the Pericote dance from Llanes.

Contents

That ancient part of history which is Spain is often referred to as "the bull's skin", because that is the shape of Spain on the map. The aim of this book is to present a detailed and comprehensive picture of a fragment of that "bull's skin", and to help this it includes a number of spectacular photographs. The Editor will be well satisfied if he has succeeded in giving you a deeper and better knowledge of Spain.

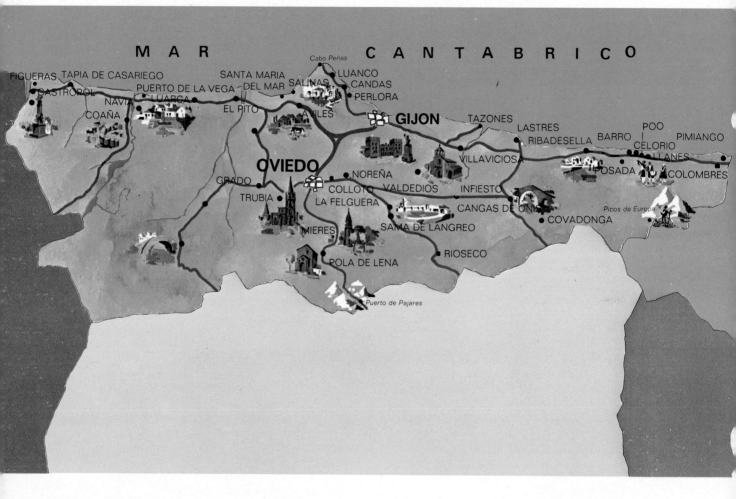

MAR CANTABRICO

FIGUERAS TAPIA DE CASARIEGO
CASTROPOL
NAVIA
COAÑA
LUARCA
PUERTO DE LA VEGA
EL PITO
SANTA MARIA DEL MAR
SALINAS
AVILES
Cabo Peñas
LUANCO
CANDAS
PERLORA
GIJON
TAZONES
LASTRES
RIBADESELLA
BARRO
POO
CELORIO
LLANES
PIMIANGO
COLOMBRES
POSADA
OVIEDO
GRADO
TRUBIA
NOREÑA
COLLOTO
LA FELGUERA
VALDEDIOS
VILLAVICIOSA
INFIESTO
CANGAS DE ONIS
COVADONGA
Picos de Europa
MIERES
SAMA DE LANGREO
RIOSECO
POLA DE LENA
Puerto de Pajares

TODO
MCMLXIX

The printing of this book was completed in the workshops of FISA - Industrias Gráficas, Palaudarias, 26 - Barcelona (Spain)